NIGHT JOURNAL

A Notebook for Nighttime:
Thoughts, Concerns
Ideas and Dreams

Volume 1

• DATES: _____ •

Blazing Fields Press

Night is the other half of life, and the better half.

Johann Wolfgang von Goethe

Night Journal, Volume 1

Copyright © Blazing Fields Press

All rights reserved. No part of this publication may be reproduced, distributed, or transmitted in any form or by any means, including photocopying, recording, or other electronic or mechanical methods, without the prior written permission of the publisher, except in the case of brief quotations embodied in critical reviews and certain other noncommercial uses permitted by copyright law.

ISBN: 1724200631
ISBN-13: 978-1724200631

Date:_____ Time:_____

Date:_____ Time:_____

Date:_____ Time:_____

Date:_____ Time:_____

Date:_____ Time:_____

Date:_____ Time:_____

Date:_____ Time:_____

Date:_____ Time:_____

Date:_____ Time:_____

Date:_____ Time:_____

Date:_____ Time:_____

Date:_____ Time:_____

Date:_____ Time:_____

Date:_____ Time:_____

Date:_____ Time:_____

Date:_____ Time:_____

Date:_____ Time:_____

Date:_____ Time:_____

Date:_____ Time:_____

Date:_____ Time:_____

Date:_____ Time:_____

Date:_____ Time:_____

Date:_____ Time:_____

Date:_____ Time:_____

Date:_____ Time:_____

Date:_____ Time:_____

Date:_____ Time:_____

Date:_____ Time:_____

Date:_____ Time:_____

Date:_____ Time:_____

Date:_____ Time:_____

Date:_____ Time:_____

Date:_____ Time:_____

Date:_____ Time:_____

Date:_____ Time:_____

Date:_____ Time:_____

Date:_____ Time:_____

Date:_____ Time:_____

Date:_____ Time:_____

Date:_____ Time:_____

Date:_____ Time:_____

Date:_____ Time:_____

Date:_____ Time:_____

Date:_____ Time:_____

Date:_____ Time:_____

Date:_____ Time:_____

Date:_____ Time:_____

Date:_____ Time:_____

Date:_____ Time:_____

Date:_____ Time:_____

Date:_____ Time:_____

Date:_____ Time:_____

Date:_____ Time:_____

Date:_____ Time:_____

Date:_____ Time:_____

Date:_____ Time:_____

Date:_____ Time:_____

Date:_____ Time:_____

Date:_____ Time:_____

Date:_____ Time:_____

Date:_____ Time:_____

Date:_____ Time:_____

Date:_____ Time:_____

Date:_____ Time:_____

Date:_____ Time:_____

Date:_____ Time:_____

Date:_____ Time:_____

Date:_____ Time:_____

Date:_____ Time:_____

Date:_____ Time:_____

Date:_____ Time:_____

Date:_____ Time:_____

Date:_____ Time:_____

Date:_____ Time:_____

Date:_____ Time:_____

Date:_____ Time:_____

Date:_____ Time:_____

Date:_____ Time:_____

Date:_____ Time:_____

Date:_____ Time:_____

Date:_____ Time:_____

Date:_____ Time:_____

Date:_____ Time:_____

Date:_____ Time:_____

Date:_____ Time:_____

Date:_____ Time:_____

Date:_____ Time:_____

Date:_____ Time:_____

Date:_____ Time:_____

Date:_____ Time:_____

Date:_____ Time:_____

Date:_____ Time:_____

Date:_____ Time:_____

Date:_____ Time:_____

Date:_____ Time:_____

Date:_____ Time:_____

Date:_____ Time:_____

Date:_____ Time:_____

Date:_____ Time:_____

Date:_____ Time:_____

Need More Space?

go to Amazon.com for

NIGHT JOURNAL
A Notebook for Nighttime Thoughts, Concerns, Ideas and Dreams
Volumes 2 - 6

For a larger layout check out

NIGHT REFLECTIONS JOURNAL
An 8"x10" journal for nighttime writing

For all our products visit us at

BlazingFields.com

Blazing Fields Press

Made in the USA
Columbia, SC
09 November 2021